LONDON COLLEGE OF MUSIC EXAMINATIONS

Grade Four

Classical Guitar Playing

Compiled by
Tony Skinner, Raymond Burley and Amanda Cook
on behalf of

The Specialists in Guitar Education

RGT®

Registry of Guitar Tutors

Printed and bound in Great Britain

A CIP record for this publication is available from the British Library
ISBN: 978-1-905908-14-1

Published by Registry Publications

Registry Mews, Wilton Rd, Bexhill, Sussex, TN40 1HY

Cover artwork by Danielle Croft. Design by JAK Images.
Music engraving by Alan J Brown, Chaz Hart and Dmitry Milovanov.

Compiled for LCM Exams by

www.RGT.org

INTRODUCTION

This publication is part of a progressive series of ten handbooks, primarily intended for candidates considering taking the London College Of Music examinations in classical guitar playing. However, given each handbook's wide content of musical repertoire and associated educational material, the series provides a solid foundation of musical education for any classical guitar student – whether intending to take an examination or not. Whilst the handbooks can be used for independent study, they are ideally intended as a supplement to individual or group tuition.

Examination entry

An examination entry form is provided at the rear of each handbook. This is the only valid entry form for the London College Of Music classical guitar examinations. Please note that *if the entry form is detached and lost, it will not be replaced under any circumstances* and the candidate will be required to obtain a replacement handbook to obtain another entry form. For candidates making online entries for classical guitar examinations, the handbook entry form must still be completed and must be submitted by post before the entry deadline to:

UK and Ireland entries: LCM Exams, University of West London, St Mary's Road, Ealing, London, W5 5RF, UK.

Entries not from the UK and Ireland: the completed entry form should be sent to your local LCM Exams Representative.

Editorial information

Examination performances must be from this handbook edition. All performance pieces should be played in full, including all repeats shown; the pieces have been edited specifically for examination use, with all non-required repeat markings omitted. Tempos, fingering and dynamic markings are for general guidance only and need not be rigidly adhered to, providing an effective musical result is achieved. In some pieces such markings are kept to a minimum to allow candidates to display individual interpretation; the omission of editorial dynamic markings does not in any way imply that dynamic variation should be absent from a performance.

Pick-hand fingering is normally shown on the stem side of the notes:
p = thumb; *i* = index finger; *m* = middle finger; *a* = third finger.

Fret-hand fingering is shown with the numbers 1 2 3 4, normally to the left of the notehead.
0 indicates an open string.

String numbers are shown in a circle, normally below the note. For example, ⑥ = 6th string.

Finger-shifts are indicated by a small horizontal dash before the left-hand finger number.

For example, 2 followed by -2 indicates that the 2nd finger can stay on the same string but move to another fret as a *guide finger*. The finger-shift sign should not be confused with a *slide* or *glissando* (where a longer dash joins two noteheads).

Slurs are indicated by a curved line between two notes of differing pitch. These should not be confused with *ties* (where two notes of the same pitch are joined by a curved line in order to increase the duration of the first note).

Full barrés (covering 5 or 6 strings with the first finger) are shown by a capital B, followed by a Roman numeral to indicate the fret position of the barré. *Half barrés* (covering 2 to 4 strings) are shown like this: ½B, followed by a Roman numeral to indicate the fret position of the half barré. For example, ½BI indicates a half barré at the first fret. A dotted line will indicate the duration for which the barré should be held.

Harmonics are shown with a diamond-shaped notehead. The fret at which they are to be played will be shown above each note, e.g. H12 for 12th fret, and the string number will be shown. On the stave, harmonics are placed at the pitch of the fretted note above which they are played – rather than the pitch at which they sound.

Arpeggiated chords, that are rolled or strummed, are indicated by a vertical wavy line to the left of the chord.

TECHNICAL WORK

The examiner will select some of the scales, arpeggios and chords shown on the following pages and ask the candidate to play them from memory. Scales and arpeggios should be played ascending and descending, i.e. from the lowest note to the highest and back again, without a pause and without repeating the top note. Chords should be played ascending only, and sounded string by string, starting with the lowest (root) note. To achieve a legato (i.e. smooth and over-ringing) sound, the whole chord shape should be fretted and kept on during playing. Chords and arpeggios should be played tirando, i.e. using free strokes.

At this grade, candidates may be asked to play a major chord with ANY root note. The chord shapes shown overleaf use 'transpositional' shapes, i.e. they can be transposed to other pitches by using the same fingering starting from a different fret. Where a transpositional shape is written in C it can be transposed along the fifth string by starting on the following frets: 4th fret for C♯/D♭, 5th fret for D, 6th fret for D♯/E♭, 7th fret for E, 8th fret for F, 9th fret for F♯/G♭. Where a transpositional shape is written in G it can be transposed along the sixth string by starting on the following frets: 4th fret for G♯/A♭, 5th fret for A, 6th fret for A♯/B♭, 7th fret for B.

To allow for flexibility in teaching approaches, the fingering suggestions provided are not compulsory and alternative systematic fingerings, that are musically effective, will be accepted. Suggested tempos are for general guidance only; slightly slower or faster performances will be acceptable, providing that the tempo is evenly maintained.

Overall, the examiner will be listening for accurate, even and clear playing. A maximum of 15 marks may be awarded in this section of the examination.

Recommended right hand fingering and tempo

Scales:	alternating *im* or *ma*	96 minim beats per minute
Arpeggios:	*pimaima* (reverse descending)	76 minim beats per minute
Chords:	*p* on all bass strings *ima* on treble strings	132 minim beats per minute

---

Key Study

The Key Study links the introduction of a new key to the performance of a short melodic theme from a piece by a well-known composer. The purpose is to make the learning of scales relevant to practical music-making and therefore memorable, as well as providing the opportunity to play music outside the standard guitar repertoire.

The examiner may request the candidate to play any, or all, of the scales within the Key Study. The examiner will also ask for a performance of ONE of the melodic themes of *the candidate's* choice. Tempo marking and fingering are for guidance only and need not be rigidly adhered to, providing an effective musical performance is achieved. The examiner will be listening, and awarding marks, for evidence of melodic phrasing and shaping, as well as for accuracy and clarity.

The Key Study must be played entirely from memory.

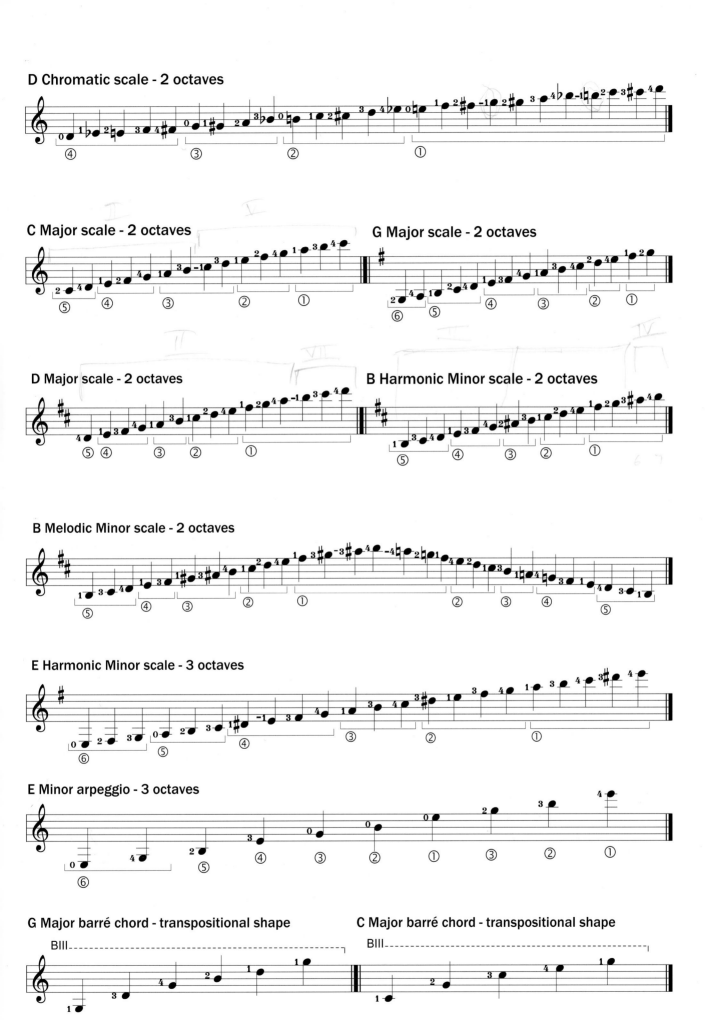

Key Study

The examiner will request a selection of the scales below,
plus ONE melodic theme *of the candidate's choice.*

Eb Major scale - 2 Octaves   **C Harmonic Minor scale - 2 octaves**

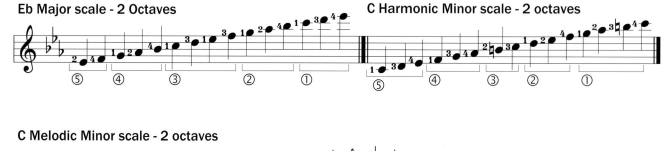

C Melodic Minor scale - 2 octaves

Melodic theme - Option One

Grand March
From Aida

Giuseppe Verdi
(1813 - 1901)

6

Melodic theme - Option Two

Waltz
From The Merry Widow

Franz Lehár
(1870 - 1948)

PERFORMANCE_____

Candidates should play *three* pieces. The programme should be balanced, with some contrasting pieces to demonstrate the candidate's range.

A maximum of 60 marks may be awarded in this section of the examination - i.e. up to 20 marks for each performance. Fingering and tempo markings are for general guidance only and do not need to be adhered to strictly. All repeat markings should be followed.

Performance Tips

Lady Fugger's Dance *(Neusiedler)*:

- This piece was written by Augsburg-based lutenist Melchior Neusiedler (born 1531). The Fugger's were a very wealthy family in Augsburg, Germany and important patrons of the arts; they had an important collection of musical instruments including around 140 lutes.

- For clarity, this lute piece has been arranged here for guitar in two voices, although a third middle voice does enter from time to time; where this occurs (such as in bars 4 and 8) the lower voice bass notes should be allowed to ring on as dotted minims. The piece consists of three 4-bar sections, each of which is followed by a 'division' (i.e. a more elaborate variation).

Aria *(Kellner)*:

- David Kellner was an organist and lutenist born in Leipzig around 1670. This piece was originally written for lute. To capture the style of the piece it is important to maintain an even tempo, and give due attention to the timing of the many dotted notes that give the piece its distinctive rhythmic character.

- Care should be taken to ensure the full note values, particularly in the bars containing syncopated rhythms (indicated by the use of ties). Due to the harmonic overlapping that was so prevalent in baroque lute music it is also particularly important to retain the full durations of the inner (middle) voice lines, which can be easily cut short if due attention is not paid to this.

Allegretto *(Sor)*:

- Fernando Sor (born Spain 1778) is widely regarded as one of the most influential classical guitarists of all time. He composed several hundred pieces for guitar, ranging from student pieces to concert works.

- This piece, taken from Sor's collection of 24 exercises Op.35, is often referred to as 'Study in B Minor'. The piece begins with a B minor barré chord played at the 2nd fret. Care should be taken throughout to ensure that the accompaniment never overpowers the melody notes (shown with upward stems). Occasionally some melody notes (e.g. in bar 32) cannot be sustained for their full written value.

Allegro *(Carcassi)*:

- Matteo Carcassi (born Italy 1792) was one of the 19th century's finest guitarists. He also composed large numbers of pieces for the student repertoire. This piece is taken from his '25 Melodic and Progressive Studies Opus 60'.

- As the title suggests, this piece should be played at quite a fast tempo. Sufficient practice and careful attention to fingering will help ensure that there are no undue gaps between chord changes. The bass line should be played strongly enough to be heard clearly.

Etude in E Minor *(Tárrega)*:

- Spanish guitarist Francisco Tárrega (born 1852) is often called 'the father of the modern classical guitar' due to his great influence on guitar technique and repertoire.

- This study in the key of E minor is very much in the Romantic vein. The melody is on the first string throughout and should be well-defined with a full, but not overpowering, tone. A wide finger stretch (from the 3rd to the 7th fret) is required in bar 12, and care should be taken not to release the G bass note before the end of this bar.

Sea Prelude *(Hart)*:

- British guitarist and composer Chaz Hart (born 1948) is an examiner in guitar playing. He has recorded several instrumental albums, and has composed numerous works for classical guitar including a guitar concerto.

- The sixth string must be tuned down a whole tone to D in order to play this piece. The opening bars involve the repeated use of first finger glissando: the notes between the two principal notes should be allowed to sound. The dynamic markings and tempo variations should be closely followed to capture the mood of the piece. Harmonics are used in the final bar: first at the 12th fret, and then at the 7th fret for the final pair of notes.

Pamplona *(Lindsey-Clark)*:

- British guitarist Vincent Lindsey-Clark (born 1956) is a prolific composer of pieces for the student repertoire. This piece is taken from his 'Simply Spanish' collection. The key signature is A minor, although in this typical Spanish style the harmonic emphasis is on the dominant chord (E major).

- You'll notice there are two time signatures: $\frac{6}{8}$ and $\frac{3}{4}$ – the rhythms alternate through much of the piece. The opening bar (and some later bars) features spread chords – these can be played by using the back of the right hand index finger.

Seashore Parade (Skinner):

- British guitarist and music educator Tony Skinner (born 1960) has composed many pieces for classical guitar and has written over 60 music education books.

- In order to achieve a warm tone the piece is fingered to commence in 9th position. The tempo should be regular with the repeated bass notes generating a walking effect, but never overpowering the melody. Harmonics on the 2nd and 4th strings are played at the 7th fret in bars 16, 22 and 25.

Cherry *(Couch)*:

- New Zealand-born recording artist and concert guitarist John Couch (born 1976) has been resident in Australia for many years and has composed many pieces for student repertoire.

- The composer advises: "Take care to play the accompaniment lightly and to bring the melody out clearly. When played rhythmically (heavy soft soft), the phrasing should come naturally. Most of the melody is on the first string and glissando could be used to help connect the melody notes in a legato fashion. A careful approach to the position changes will facilitate an accurate performance."

Lady Fugger's Dance

Melchior Neusiedler
(1531 - 1590)

Aria

David Kellner
(1670 – 1748)

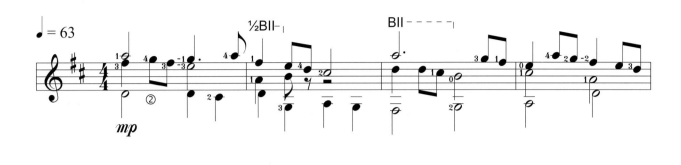

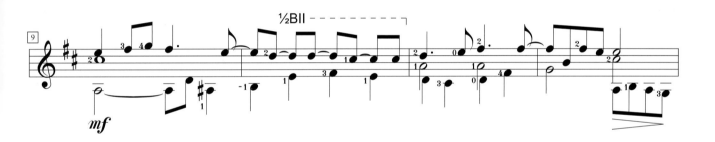

Allegretto Op. 35 No. 22

Fernando Sor
(1778 - 1839)

Allegro Op.60 No. 7

Matteo Carcassi
(1792 - 1853)

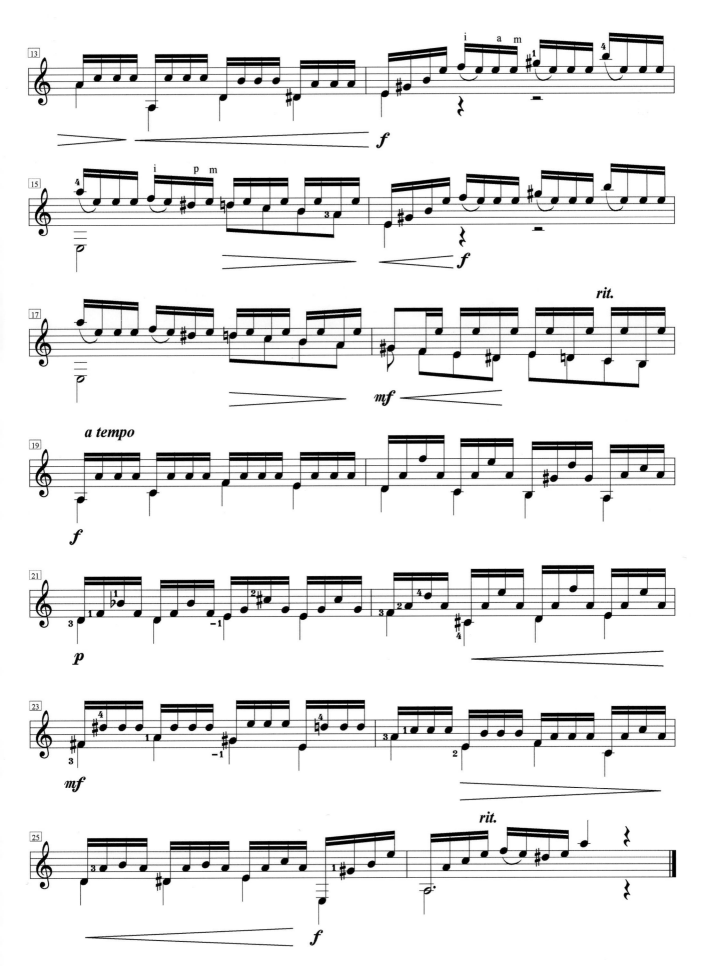

Etude in E Minor

Francisco Tárrega
(1852 - 1909)

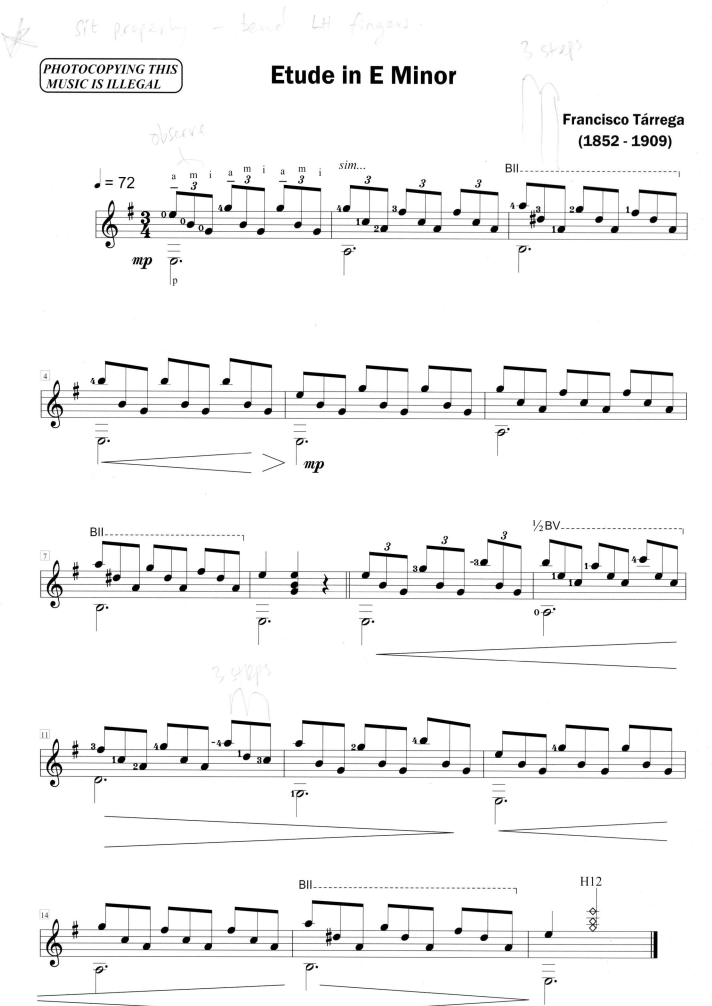

16

Sea Prelude

Chaz Hart
(1948 -)

17

Pamplona

Vincent Lindsey-Clark
(1956 –)

19

Seashore Parade

Tony Skinner
(1960 -)

Cherry

John Couch
(1976 –)

VIVA VOCE

I n this section of the examination candidates will be engaged in a short discussion to enable the examiner to assess the candidate's understanding of musical fundamentals and their responses to the pieces played. A maximum of 7 marks may be awarded.

Candidates should be able to name, and explain the meaning of, all notational elements in the music performed in the Performance component of the exam including key and time signatures, accidentals, dynamics, articulation markings and any additional markings. In addition, candidates should be able to:

- describe the mood and character of pieces using appropriate descriptive terminology (e.g. 'fast and lively', 'gentle and flowing', 'like a dance', etc.) and identify contrasts of mood within pieces and describe any pictorial or descriptive element of the music;

- identify intervals up to and including an octave by numerical value only (e.g. 'fourth', 'seventh', etc.);

- demonstrate basic knowledge of composers of the music performed, including their nationality and approximate dates;

- explain which is their favourite piece and why, and discuss their approaches to learning the pieces and identify any particular difficulties (musical or technical) that were encountered;

- demonstrate a basic understanding of the workings of the guitar and name its principal constituent parts.

Below are some examples of the type of questions that the examiner may ask at this grade. Note that these are examples only; the list is by no means exhaustive and candidates should not simply learn these answers by rote. The wording and phrasing of the questions may vary even when the same topic is involved.

Question: What is this interval? (Examiner points to C and A.)
Answer: It is a sixth.

Question: Explain the meaning of this. (Examiner points to 'cresc. poco a poco' in *Pamplona*)
Answer: Crescendo little by little - meaning get louder very gradually.

Question: What key is this piece in? (*Seashore Parade*)
Answer: A major.

Question: What is the time signature of this piece? (*Lady Fugger's Dance*)
Answer: It is 'cut common time', which means two minim beats per bar.

Question: Tell me something about the mood and character of this piece. (*Lady Fugger's Dance*)
Answer: It is quite bright and dance-like. The variations that occur after every 4 bar section help give it a real sense of momentum.

Question: What do you know about the composer of this piece? (*Sea Prelude*)
Answer: He is a modern British composer.

Question: Was there anything about this piece that was difficult to learn? (*Pamplona*)
Answer: Because of the numerous changes from $\frac{3}{4}$ to $\frac{6}{8}$ it was hard at first to get the timing right; I needed to practise carefully so as not to rush the $\frac{3}{4}$ bars.

Question: How do you get a clean sound when fretting notes?
Answer: By pressing with the tips of the fingertips close to the fretwire.

Some useful information relating to this section of the examination is provided below. Candidates lacking knowledge in this general area are advised to study for the London College of Music music theory examinations, using suitable music theory books, worksheets and musical dictionaries. Advice and tuition from an experienced teacher would undoubtedly prove helpful.

Major and minor key signatures

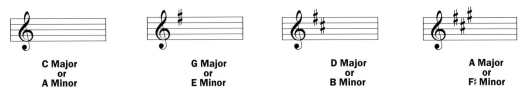

Candidates should be able to identify whether a piece is in the major key or its relative minor key. This is often indicated by the presence of an accidental on the leading note of the minor key. For example, G# in the key of A minor, D# in the key of E minor and A# in the key of B minor. Candidates should also examine the first and final chord, or bass note, to help establish the tonality.

Intervals

Candidates will be expected to identify by numeric value (e.g. 6th) any intervals up to and including an octave that occur in the music performed. Examples in the key of C major are given below.

You can work out any interval number by counting the number of lines and spaces between two notes – making sure to include the first and final notes of the interval in your count.

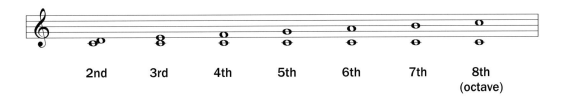

Time signatures

The time signatures that occur at this grade are:

$\frac{2}{2}$ = 2 minim beats per bar. Also known as 'cut common time' and indicated by ¢. *Simple duple time.*

$\frac{3}{4}$ = 3 crotchet beats per bar. *Simple triple time.*

$\frac{4}{4}$ = 4 crotchet beats per bar. This is also indicated by C. *Simple quadruple time.*

$\frac{6}{8}$ = 6 quavers, but with 2 dotted crotchet beats per bar. *Compound duple time.*

Common terms and signs

Candidates should have an understanding of any terms and signs that appear in the music performed. Some examples are given below.

>	accent
D.C. al Fine	repeat from the beginning up to the point marked *Fine* (the end)
sim. (simile.)	continue in a like manner
dolce	tenderly (with a sweet tone)

Tenuto sign. To be held for its full value and slightly emphasised.

Repeat sign. Play from the previous 2 vertical dots, or, in their absence, from the beginning.

First time ending. On the first playing, play the notes below this box.

Second time ending. On the second playing, omit the first time ending and play from this bar.

Dynamics

ppp	*pp*	*p*	*mp*	*mf*	*f*	*ff*	*fff*
pianissimo very soft	piano soft	mezzo-piano medium soft	mezzo-forte medium loud		forte loud	fortissimo very loud	

cresc. (crescendo) – getting louder

decresc. (decrescendo) – getting softer

dim. (diminuendo) – gradually becoming softer

Tempo terms

Rall. (rallentando)	becoming gradually slower
Rit. (ritenuto)	held back
poco rit.	held back a little
⌢ *Fermata*	pause (lengthen the note)
Allargando	getting slower with a bigger tone
Allegro	fast
Allegretto	fairly fast (not as fast as *Allegro*)
Allegro vivace	quick and lively
a tempo	revert to previous tempo
♩ = 120	metronome marking (e.g. 120 crotchet beats per minute)

Candidates should also refer to the Performance Notes and Introduction of this handbook which include descriptions of specialist guitar signs.

SIGHT READING

The examiner will show you the sight reading test and allow you just a short time to look over it before performing it. A maximum of 10 marks may be awarded in this section of the examination. The table below shows the range of the piece:

Length	Keys	Time signatures	Note values	Fingerboard positions
8 bars	Major: F, C, G, D Minor: D, A, E, B	2 3 4 6 4 4 4 8	o ♩. ♩ ♩ ♩ ♪ ♪ ♪	1st / 2nd / 3rd

SIGHT READING TIPS

1. Always check the key and time signature BEFORE you start to play.

2. Once you have identified the key it is helpful to remember that the notes will all come from the key scale.

3. Before you start to play, quickly scan through the piece and check any notes or rhythms that you are unsure of. Where fretted bass notes occur simultaneously with melody notes, decide which left-hand fingering you will need to use.

4. Note the tempo or style marking, but be careful to play at a tempo at which you can maintain accuracy throughout.

5. Once you start to play, try and keep your eyes on the music. Avoid the temptation to keep looking at the fingerboard – that's a sure way to lose your place in the music.

6. Observe all rests and try to follow the dynamic markings.

7. If you do make an error, try not to let it affect your confidence for the rest of the piece. It is better to keep going and capture the overall shape of the piece, rather than stopping and going back to correct errors.

The following examples show the *type* of pieces that will be presented in the examination.

(ii)   Maestoso

(iii)   Allegretto

(iv)   Moderato

AURAL TESTS

A maximum of 8 marks may be awarded in this section of the examination. The tests will be played by the examiner on either guitar or piano, at the examiner's discretion. The examples below are shown in guitar notation and give a broad indication of the type of tests that will be given during the examination. Candidates wishing to view sample tests in piano notation should obtain the current LCM Exams *Specimen Aural Tests* booklet.

Rhythm tests

1a. The examiner will twice play a short harmonised piece of music in $\frac{2}{4}$, $\frac{3}{4}$, $\frac{4}{4}$ or $\frac{6}{8}$ time, similar to the examples below. During the second playing, the candidate should beat time (conduct), with a clear beat shape (conducting pattern) according to the time signature of the music, in time with the examiner's playing. The examiner will take the response only from the beat, and will not accept a verbal description of the time signature.

> **Beating time.**
> To beat time, begin with your arm out in front of you, with your hand at eye level. The first beat of each bar should be shown by a strong downwards motion of the arm. In $\frac{3}{4}$ time, move the arm to the right for beat two and return to the top of your 'triangle' for beat three. $\frac{4}{4}$ will involve a horizontal move to the left for beat two and to the right for beat three; the final fourth beat being a return upwards to your starting position. If you are left-handed, you should swap the left and right motions. $\frac{6}{8}$ time should be beat as two dotted crotchet (dotted quarter note) beats – one down and one up. $\frac{2}{4}$ time should be beat in a similar way.

1b. The examiner will twice play one phrase of the piece, lasting approximately two bars, in a single line version. The candidate should reproduce the rhythm of this phrase by tapping or clapping. Tests will contain notes no shorter than a semiquaver. Simple dotted patterns may be included. The example below is taken from the opening of the first piece.

Pitch tests

2a. The examiner will play an interval twice: first with the notes sounded successively, and then with the notes played together. The candidate should identify the interval by type and numerical value (e.g. major 7th). The test will then be repeated using a different interval. The interval will be restricted to any major, minor or perfect interval up to and including an octave. Examples are given below with a tonic note of C.

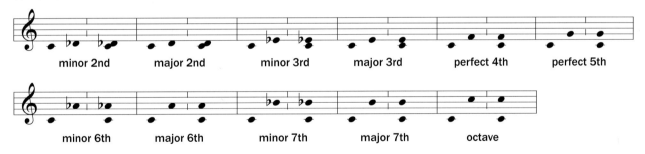

2b. The examiner will show the candidate three similar versions of a short tune. The versions will differ in pitch but not rhythm. One version will be played to the candidate twice. The candidate must state which version was played. Some examples are shown below.

Set 2

1

Set 3

Set 4

UNIVERSITY OF WEST LONDON
LONDON COLLEGE OF MUSIC EXAMINATIONS

Classical Guitar
Examination Entry Form

GRADE FOUR
or Recital Grade 4
or Level 4 Leisure Play

The standard LCM Exams music entry form is NOT valid for Classical Guitar entries.
Entry to the examination is only possible via this original form.
Photocopies of this form will not be accepted under any circumstances.

For candidates making online entries for classical guitar examinations, the handbook entry form must still be completed and must be submitted by post before the entry deadline to:
For UK and Ireland entries: LCM Exams, University of West London, St Mary's Road, Ealing, London, W5 5RF, UK.
For entries not from the UK and Ireland: the completed entry form should be sent to your local LCM Exams Representative.

Please use black ink and block capital letters when completing this form.

Circle the type of examination you wish to enter: Grade   Recital Grade   Leisure Play

SESSION (Spring/Summer/Winter): _____ YEAR:_____

Preferred Examination Centre (if known): _____
If left blank you will be examined at the nearest venue to your home address.

Candidate Details:

Candidate Name (as to appear on certificate):

_____

Candidate ID (if entered previously): _____ Date of birth: _____

Gender (M/F): _____ Ethnicity (see chart overleaf):_____

Date of birth and ethnicity details are for statistical purposes only, and are not passed on to the examiner.

☐ Tick this box if you are attaching details of particular needs requirements.

Teacher Details:

Teacher Name (as to appear on certificate): _____

Teacher Qualifications (if required on certificate): _____

LCM Teacher Code (if entered previously): _____

Address: _____

_____ Postcode: _____

Tel. No. (day): _____(evening): _____

Email Address: _____

☐ Tick this box if any details above have changed since your last LCM entry.

IMPORTANT NOTES

- It is the candidate's responsibility to have knowledge of, and comply with, the current syllabus requirements. Where candidates are entered for examinations by a teacher, the teacher must take responsibility that candidates are entered in accordance with the current syllabus requirements. Failure to carry out any of the examination requirements may lead to disqualification.

- For candidates with particular needs, a letter giving details and requests for any special requirements (e.g. enlarged sight reading), together with an official supporting document (e.g. medical certificate), should be attached.

- Examinations may be held on any day of the week, including weekends. Any appointment requests (e.g. 'prefer morning,' or 'prefer weekdays') must be made at the time of entry. **LCM Exams and its Representatives will take note of the information given; however, no guarantees can be made that all wishes can be met.**

- Submission of this entry is an undertaking to abide by the current regulations.

ETHNIC ORIGIN CLASSIFICATIONS

White
01	British
02	Irish
03	Other white background

Mixed
04	White and black Caribbean
05	White and black African
06	White and Asian
07	Other mixed background

Asian or Asian British
08	Indian
09	Pakistani
10	Bangladeshi
11	Other Asian background

Black or Black British
12	Caribbean
13	African
14	Other black background

Chinese or Other Ethnic Group
15	Chinese
16	Other
17	**Prefer not to say**

Examination Fee: £ _____

Late Entry Fee (if necessary) £ _____

Total amount submitted: £ _____

If already entered and paid on-line, tick here: _____

Cheques or postal orders should be made payable to '*University of West London*'.

A list of current fees, entry deadlines and session dates is available from LCM Exams.

Where to submit your entry form

Entries for public centres should be sent to the
**LCM Exams local examination centre representative
(NOT to the LCM Exams Head Office).**

View the LCM Exams website www.uwl.ac.uk/lcmexams
or contact the LCM Exams office (tel: 020 8231 2364 / email: lcm.exams@uwl.ac.uk)
for details of your nearest local examination centre representative.

Entries for private centres, should be sent direct to:
LCM Exams, University of West London, St Mary's Road, Ealing, London, W5 5RF

Official Entry Form